Flat Fee Freelancer

Flat Fee Freelancer

Why You Can (and Should) Triple Your Income in the Gig Economy

Stephen Poynter

Copyright © 2020 Stephen Poynter

All rights reserved.

ISBN: 979-8-6900-5329-1

Library of Congress Control Number: 2020918790

Cover designs by Courtney Whalen

Printed in the United States of America

Northernwords Press
Grand Marais, Minnesota, USA
www.northernwords.blog

What if rather than focusing on how long something took, we focused on how far we went?

— Benjamin P. Hardy

Table of Contents

Introduction	1
The Gig Economy Is Great – Until It Isn't	3
Challenge 1 – Stop Underestimating Yourself	14
Challenge 2 – Change the Way Your Clients See You	17
Hours Don't Matter	19
The Project Fee	24
Conclusion	33
Acknowledgements	37
About the Author	39
Endnotes	41

Introduction

This book is for the freelancer. For the gig economy worker. For the independent contractor. For the small-business owner, the entrepreneur, the consultant, the artist, the aspiring writer, the burnt-out tutor, and the underrated web developer. Whoever you are, if you have a valuable skill you are trying to offer to the world – if you are the type of person who can see a need individuals or businesses have, and then say with conviction (however many lingering doubts are hiding under the surface), "Pick me – I am the one who can meet this need, and here's why," then this book is for you. It's for all of us.

We need to hear this book's message because our livelihoods depend on it. I don't mean to exaggerate in saying so. I've met a lot of freelancers (being one myself), and I must say I have been impressed with what I've seen. There is so much talent, so much genuine passion, so many countless hours (and years!) of hard work represented in this large and diverse community. And so much being-broke-and-afraid-of-going-more-broke.

If you are reading this, you are probably a pretty neat person with great ideas that you put a lot of care and effort into. I commend you for that. You likely have a definitive skill set or product that is effective for a niche market and that you are passionate about promoting (if not, then you need to work on that first, then come back here[1]).

And if you are reading this, there is a good chance you are struggling to make ends meet. Perhaps you are wondering why that is – or if you made the right choice in being an entrepreneur in the first place.

I don't claim to be inventing anything groundbreaking or radical here. I just want to share some facts that desperately need to be heard by the freelance community, and especially those newer to it, because I want to see freelancers succeed. But it may take a radical change in our mindsets – a paradigm shift, if you will – for some of us to fully wrestle with these facts and adopt the practical changes that may be necessary.

Some of the terminology and examples used in this book come specifically from a framework of one-on-one freelancing (and may be less relevant to, say, an app-based gig that doesn't give you much control over pricing). However, I think you'll find the fundamental mindset and principles are relevant to all self-employed persons, and can help guide you as you approach big-picture decisions about how you structure your work and career.

The premises of this book are twofold, and straightforward: (1) As a freelancer, you are taking on incredible levels of expenses and risks, which are otherwise typically borne by employers, while providing at least as much value and productivity (usually more so) than a comparable employee, and (2) Project fees, rather than hourly rates, are usually a far superior method of structuring your compensation to reflect this.

Some of you already know all this, and may not need to read this book. Some of you may have been in the gig economy for years, scraping by with unwittingly-low hourly rates, while not recognizing how much more potential you may be leaving on the table. Some of you are new to the gig economy, or are aspiring to wed yourself to that prestigious, lucrative title, and, oh boy – you have no idea what you are getting yourself into…

The Gig Economy Is Great – Until It Isn't

The gig economy isn't a novel idea. After all, self-driven work and independent negotiation is how the majority of people operated before the industrial age.[2] The single-employer-provides-all model is a relatively recent phenomenon, and not necessarily a bad one at that; however, it is the framework most of us and our parents have grown up accustomed to – and we can't necessarily bring our expectations from that framework into the freelance world.

What *is* new is the recent resurgence of the gig economy and the way we do it. Emboldened by the wonders of the internet age and smartphone apps, we have rapidly expanded the ways we work and consume. The gig economy is heralded as representing the best of the 21st century: connecting people through decentralized platforms of trust, unlimited flexibility and potential, harnessing the power of user-generated data, leveling the playing field and enabling anyone to be an entrepreneur, and real-time and customized solutions for customer needs.

And in many cases, it has delivered on these promises. Meaningful stats on freelancing are inherently hard to come by since the gig world is fragmented, self-reported, and usually part-time or seasonal; however, the majority of freelancers report being satisfied with their jobs (showing a similar satisfaction rate as employees).[3] They do report slightly higher rates of satisfaction when it comes to work/life balance.[4] There are many freelancers who report making over six figures in the process – in fact, around 40% of those who do freelance work using the digital marketplace without having any outside employment report this level of income, according to PYMNTS' most recently-published Gig Economy Index report.[5]

However, this is far from the full picture. That 40% with a six-figure income, like many such lauded figures, must be taken with a large grain of salt (or several grains). It only looks at those who do not have any outside employment, which is going to exclude by definition less successful freelancers that need to rely on traditional employment for stability, as most do (a full 38% of those same PYMNTS respondents – those without outside employment – had a graduate degree). Even within this segment of freelancers, this doesn't tell us anything about the other 60% who make under $100k (from what we will see below, it doesn't necessarily look too good for them).

By comparison, a Morning Consult survey found about only 14% of *all* self-identified gig economy participants reported six-figure incomes, which is barely higher than that of the overall workforce.[6] As will be seen later, $100k in freelance income isn't anywhere near comparable to $100k in employment income. An income distribution for gig economy participants that at face value is only slightly higher than that of the overall workforce is in reality one that is much worse.

Moreover, all cross-sectional polls such as these will greatly under-report the experiences of those who fail at freelancing due to survivorship bias: those who do well in the gig economy have staying power and are much more likely, at any given point in time, to be "around" when a poll of freelancers is taken, whereas the countless people who give the gig economy an attempt and aren't able to last in it are less likely to be represented.

Flat Fee Freelancer

There is more troubling news for the gig-topia seeker according to the Federal Reserve's 2018 "Report on the Economic Well-Being of U.S. Households": a full 58 percent of workers who participate in the gig economy as their primary (though not necessarily sole) source of income reported they would have trouble handling a $400 unexpected expense, vs. 38 percent of people who don't do any gig work.[7] Of course, there are many people who are in financial straits and turn to the gig economy for some supplemental income, so the cause-effect can go both ways, but this figure is looking specifically at those freelancers (about one out of five) who are relying on the gig economy as their primary income source – and it doesn't look very promising.

Uber took off with a bang in 2011, due to its brilliant yet simple strategy – allow drivers and riders to carpool together through an on-demand, efficient platform. It led to a lot of customers getting better rides, and a lot of drivers being able to make some extra cash on their own schedule. But many drivers have felt left in the dust, and justifiably so: it turns out that after accounting for all work expenses, as of 2018 the equivalent average wage for Uber drivers was estimated to be $9.21/hour, less than the minimum wage at the time in 13 of the 20 major urban areas which it served.[8] This may just be a hint as to why the average Uber driver only sticks around for 3 months.

I'm not saying that Uber is bad or that they should be singled out (at least not for this reason alone). But it is a prime example of the paradoxical paradigm of the new economy, one that delivers unique, meaningful, and flexible connections between entrepreneurs and customers, yet drives out its users from the platforms that promised to enable them; one that loudly gushes on how you can quit your job, but doesn't tell you how much that will cost you; one that offers many real success stories, but far too often overpromises and underperforms.

In the end, the picture that emerges is one where there are some freelancers that are realizing the dreams that freelancing promised, while many others struggle severely. There are definitely many freelancers that are doing well, especially in high-paying fields such as computer coding and finance, as the share of gig workers with highly-specialized skills has grown.[9] However, that is not the experience everyone has. If you do not have a specialized skill set, and/or do not know what you are getting yourself into, then you are very unlikely to do well.

I'm not against the freelance economy; as a whole, I'm very thankful for it. But if you are going to be part of it, I want you to do it well. What I'm against is walking into it naively, and ruining your life in the process. The flexibility, autonomy, creative potential, and financial reward are there – if you know how to do it right. If you don't – well, that's when the dream turns into a nightmare.

Why Employers Love Freelancers

There's something else to bear in mind. In addition to the opportunities created by the digital age and the unique benefits workers and consumers find in the freelancing model, there is another undercurrent fueling the flight to freelancing: businesses' quest for ever-expanding profit margins.

Over the past few decades, US companies have been able to pull on a powerful combination of levers resulting in nearly doubling their profit margins: falling interest rates, ever-lower tax rates, reduced labor/union power, technological advances, and reduced regulatory scrutiny.[10] The "labor share" of the economy, or the portion of economic output in which workers share (in the form of total compensation, including non-wage benefits), has declined significantly during this time:[11]

Flat Fee Freelancer

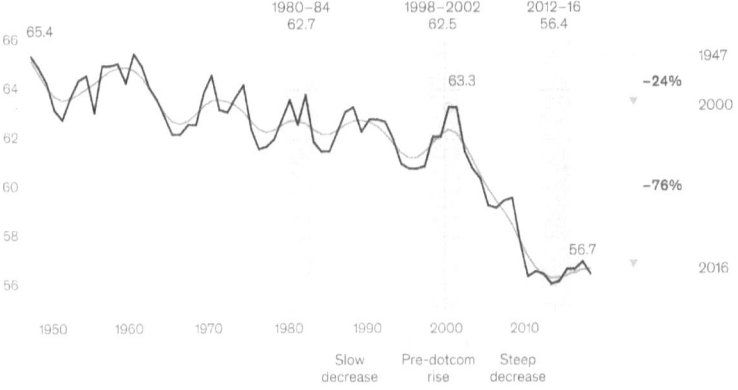

These levers that have enabled this shift of output from labor to capital can only be pulled so far, and many are at risk of leveling off or even reversing. While these trends have already resulted in a significantly lower share of the economy going to labor, corporations are always looking for ways to save on costs, and are likely thrilled at the prospects of two growing trends that can in some cases eliminate the need for employment altogether: freelancing and automation. All else being equal, a loss for labor is a win for capital – so if you find yourself on the labor side of things, don't get too excited about ditching the title of employee, at least until you make sure you aren't going to end up holding the short end of the stick.

Why might your employer like the idea of you becoming an independent contractor? Same reason a parent might be relieved when their grown kid finally moves out of the house! An employer only has to give an independent contractor a check, whereas there are countless obligations they have to employees besides base pay.

Ask any employer, and they could give you a lengthy laundry list of things they pay for on behalf of their employees. These will include benefits provided directly to you as an employee, costs borne that you don't have to see, and a safety net of liabilities your employer takes on for you, which at least in the US often include:

Base pay [notice we aren't done with the list yet]

Paid time off: vacation days, paid holidays, sick days, parental leave, personal leave, volunteer time off, bereavement leave

Daily paid breaks

Overtime pay

Bonuses, profit sharing, and/or stock options

Personal insurances: Life insurance, health insurance, disability insurance, dental insurance, vision insurance, unemployment insurance, Health Savings Accounts. Each of these items should really deserve its own line – they are huge!

Business insurances: Liability, property, catastrophe/business continuity, key person life, etc.

FSAs: Flexible Spending Accounts (which can allow you to save big on healthcare and dependent care expenses) are not available to self-employed individuals.

Charitable giving matches or similar programs

Management/training: Maybe some view their manager as an enemy, but most of the time employees wouldn't be half as productive or satisfied in their work without managers and systems there to train, educate, encourage, and correct them along the way.

Flat Fee Freelancer

Continuing education/conferences

Higher education reimbursement

Perks such as meals at client events and travel

Company lunches, parties, and team-building events

Childcare benefits

Gym memberships or discounts

Birthday/holiday/work anniversary gifts

Tax accounting (i.e. tax withholding and forms)

Smartphone and/or phone service plan

Laptops, printers, and other hardware

Software and internet service: Once you quit your job, Microsoft Office doesn't magically show up on your laptop anymore; you have to pay for it. Up here in northern Minnesota, power outages are frequent and internet access isn't always a given. The dream of working on a laptop at a coffee shop loses some of its charm when you realize the shop invested about as much in their internet routers as they did in their bathroom décor (and don't be fooled by the WiFi passcode – everyone else has the same passcode and can see your business activity if they want to).

Physical needs and supplies: Building, parking, snacks, desk, air conditioning, ergonomic chairs, printers that actually have ink, staplers that get replaced when they disappear, bathrooms with plumbing you don't ever see the bill for, and if you're lucky, perhaps even yoga rooms and ping pong and beer – in other words, your employer likely provides a quiet, safe, climate-controlled, reliable, and positive environment with all the tools and amenities needed to be productive at (and perhaps even enjoy) your work.

Payroll/Self-employment (a.k.a. FICA) taxes: Employers split the burden with you, so you pay only 7.65% as an employee, vs. 15.3% as an independent contractor. That adds up!

Work retirement plan (e.g. 401(k), 403(b), pension, etc.): Employers often provide for both the plan administration and employer contributions.

Payroll processing/invoicing: That automatic recurring direct deposit starts looking really nice when you are instead dealing with mailing and keeping track of invoices, checks, and overdue payments that don't show up (trust me, you will deal with a lot of the latter).

HR/networking: In my former job, there was this thing called an HR department. I love HR departments! An entire department working around the clock, mainly devoted to one cause – to take care of you and make your life easier. Sounds nice. They also take care of identifying other talent and, more broadly, the company establishes a network of employees and contractors and vendors that you can go to whenever you have a need. A network like that takes a lot of effort and time to build from scratch!

Marketing: In my former job, there was also this thing called a Marketing department. I love marketing departments! They bring in the clients, and I get to focus on doing my job. Without marketing, you don't have clients, and without clients, you don't have a business.

Tech support: In my former job, there was another thing called a Tech department. I love Tech departments! They would literally run to my rescue whenever needed (i.e. hardware not working, Windows crashing, file went missing, etc.) which is to say, usually at least 10 times before 8:30 am.

Compliance/legal costs and support: And in my former job, there was this thing called a Compliance department. I love Compliance departments! They might be popular targets for scorn, but clearly anyone who doesn't value a compliance department has never had to fill out paperwork or go through registration or licensing processes on their own, without anyone there to tell them when you need forms and which forms are needed and where to get the forms and how often to get them and how to fill them out and what happens if you don't and who's in trouble if you don't and how many thousands of dollars or years in jail happen if something goes wrong.

A separate, designated work environment: This is a less tangible benefit, and hence often overlooked, but it can be a huge one. In a traditional employment situation, you normally have a place of employment (that's not your house), work equipment and notes (that aren't brought home), a work phone number (that's not your personal number), and a work email (that you don't see until you clock in). When you are a freelancer, all this is brought home, into your personal life and personal space and personal time. You are never really off the clock. You can't leave your work problems at work – they follow you around. "Work" is not a separate entity you can attend to with portions of your life in exchange for compensation, then have the rest of your life totally at your own disposal. This doesn't mean you never have time for other pursuits, but there's the nagging "work" part of your brain that is always turned on, always listening for that buzz signaling the client returning your email, or trying to work out a PR mess you got into inadvertently, or wondering whether you should start revising that RFP tonight after you get back from your kid's soccer practice. You were told that in the gig economy you get to set your own hours, which is true – but were you told you would never clock out?

Stability of Pay: This is by far one of the biggest benefits an employer provides. Compensation isn't just about the level of pay, but its predictability. For example, which would you rather have: $52,000 paid in equal, guaranteed $2,000 installments every other week for a year? Or $52,000 paid out randomly over the course of a year, with some of it lumped together and some long gaps of unknown duration without any pay (and some payments that likely never end up arriving at all – about 1 out of 8 payments, actually, as we will see later)? Those $52,000, while on paper looking like identical amounts, in practice are much different. With one of them, it is a lot harder to pay a mortgage or plan capital expenditures for a business. I'll let you guess which one.

Workers' Compensation: This one is huge. And, in a more general sense, the principle it represents is huge: the employer is responsible if something goes wrong. Bad chair causing back pain? Old tool injures you? Customer unhappy and threatening to sue? Breakroom granola bars gone stale? In the traditional employment model, the employer is the one with the target on their back, and they are likely doing everything they can to make it right immediately in order to avoid further trouble or publicity. In the gig economy? You guessed it. You've got the big old fat bullseye on your back. Run into trouble? Have fun.

The Lesson

In short, an employer has got your back (granted, the extent to which they make efforts to do so varies, but the principle remains the same). They are a giant safety net. Without one, you're on your own, which honestly should be somewhat frightening. It's not something to be taken lightly.

In socialist economies, the government (usually) provides most of these safety nets – in which case you're good to go. In capitalist economies, traditionally (especially after the strengthening of labor unions in the middle of the last century), employers provide most of these safety nets – in which case you're also good to go. In the emerging gig economy … oh crap, NO ONE is providing ANY of these safety nets or benefits to you.[12] You are absolutely NOT good to go. I can't emphasize this enough. This is a huge problem.

As an independent contractor, you are taking on both a ton of expenses and a ton of risks that employers normally would take on. You MUST be compensated for that!

By definition, if you are working for pay, you are accepting money to compensate for expenses you incur and risks you take. Yet so many freelancers don't recognize the value of the added expenses and risks they incur, and hence don't expect any more compensation than an hourly figure on paper that looks similar to what they might receive as an employee. Changing this mindset is your first challenge.

Unfortunately, many clients don't fully realize this either, and they may be reluctant to pay you more than an hourly figure that on paper looks similar to what they might pay an employee. Getting your clients to pay more is challenge number two.

Challenge 1 – Stop Underestimating Yourself

Your first challenge is to recognize your own worth. Stop selling yourself short!

If you want a daunting task, try estimating and adding up dollar amounts for all the costs described in the last chapter that would apply to your line of work – you will likely be able to think of some additional ones as well. It may be eye-opening. If you are currently freelancing, what sort of base wage could you make as an employee such that, after all the other factors are included, you would be as well off as you are now? Are you actually better off now than you would be if you were making minimum wage flipping burgers for a good employer?

If not, then it's worth taking a step back and asking yourself: What are you doing? Why are you here?

Presumably, you believe (even passionately) that you actually have some important skill that adds tangible value to your clients. Do you really believe that? If so, then act like that's true! Run your business like that's true. Price your services like that's true. Or else, sooner or later, I can almost guarantee that it won't be true any longer because you *will* be flipping burgers!

How do you quantify how much your services are worth? A good place to *start* is by looking at how much you could make in wages and other compensation in your field, and make needed adjustments. We will look at a few figures for some context on that below. However, you should also consider the flip side, by looking on a case-by-case basis how much value a *client* will get from your services, which is an idea we will develop more in later chapters while on the topic of project fees.

Let's start with wages. In the US, wages and salaries on average only account for about 69% of employee compensation.[13] This might not be that surprising given all the costs we touched on in the last chapter. And as you saw in the chart in the last chapter, that employee compensation, on average, now only accounts for a little over half of the total output that each employee produces.[14]

This means that if you were to bill an hourly rate to your client, it should probably be *at least* three times higher than what you would make as a wage if you were an employee in a comparable line of work, in order to cover all your compensation and other business costs (and that's assuming you are billing for all hours you work, and getting paid for all the hours you bill, each of which is rarely the case). Many employers could attest to this; one owner of an engineering consulting business estimated that a fully-onboarded employee costs her nearly 3 times the base salary – and that doesn't even include the fixed overhead (independent of number of employees) that you need to account for as a business owner.[15]

If you would like to look into averages for your specific line of work, there are of course many free resources online that will give you an idea of base wage (I like Glassdoor), but there are also organizations such as the Bureau of Labor Statistics that can give you industry-specific data on more comprehensive measures such as total compensation and value of output per worker.[16] Many states also have their own labor market information websites where you might be able to get very localized data on compensation for your line of work.

Additionally, as a freelancer you aren't charging just to cover your compensation costs and business expenses – you need some form of additional profit in order to compensate for the liabilities you assume as your own business owner. Remember that big old target on your back? The great trade-off of being an entrepreneur is taking on that risk in the hopes of earning your own profit.

While the idea of "profit" sometimes carries a negative connotation (and sometimes deservedly so, in cases where owners pursue it at all costs and neglect their broader obligations), at root it is simply the ability to get rewarded, if you do well, for the cost and risk you took when you decided to start a business.

And some profits are absolutely necessary in order to set aside for a rainy day, as the recent recession has yet again reminded us. Otherwise, if you are only charging enough to barely scrape by when things are going well, what are you going to do when things don't go well? Nearly all businesses have some cyclicality. You'll want to still be around when that happens, in a financial sense, for your own sake, the sake of your friends and family, and for the sake of your customers.

In short, what this comes down to is fairly simple, yet cannot be overstated: what you are charging as an independent contractor is your business *revenue*; you are *not* just charging your wage. This revenue needs to be enough to cover wages, non-wage compensation, business expenses,[17] and profits.

The Society for Human Resource Management found that the median revenue generated per full-time employee (as of 2017) is about $168,000/year![18] Are you providing as much value as the typical full-time employee? If so, are you charging revenue for your business in a way that appropriately reflects that fact?

So recognize the value of what you provide. Don't hold back! Own it. Align your mindset to match the reality of what you are doing.

Provide quality, and expect appropriate payment in return. There's nothing mercenary or unjust about that. It's called common sense. It's called staying alive.

Challenge 2 – Change the Way Your Clients See You

The second challenge is to help your client see the value you provide. Now, there is the easy way and the hard way. Let's look at the hard way first.

The Hard Way

The hard way (which you are welcome to try, and which may work in some cases) is to explain to your client everything I just explained to you. Detail the expenses you incur as a contractor, the cost savings you provide them by not being their employee, the liabilities you are assuming for your efforts and the liabilities you are freeing them of by not being under their protection. Explain why you need a much higher hourly rate than a comparable employee would in order to simply break even, and negotiate what that higher hourly rate would be.

Now, as I said, this method can work, but it's messy. Messy because there is a lot of explaining involved, and you would probably much rather be spending your time productively brainstorming with your client over solutions you are building for them rather than, say, haggling over how much workers' compensation costs.

It's also messy because framing the conversation in terms of hourly rates invites a million mental comparisons. Your client will (however subconsciously) be thinking about how the hourly rate you ask for compares to what you may be expected to make at a similar job, or what he makes, or what he pays his employees, or what national averages are, or what minimum wage is, etc.

There are a lot of mental benchmarks he is likely familiar with and within which he will want to bracket you. The question of hourly rates can become a personal question (is he ruefully remembering how he sweated through college at $5/hour and, theoretically, never complained?); a tricky question (does he want to try to explain to his boss that he is paying you a higher rate [on paper] than his boss makes); a relational question (if he tries to negotiate a dollar or two down, is he implying you aren't worth quite as much as a person, or will he be too afraid to try and just turn you away); and even a political question. In short, messy.

How about the easy way?

The Easy Way
What do I suggest?

Charge a flat fee. Aka a project fee.

This avoids all the issues described above.

You don't need to convince your client of your value *per se*. The discussion isn't centered on you at all. By charging a project fee, you are doing a complete 180 and framing the conversation squarely on your client and the project or deliverable they will receive (the value to them), rather than the hours you are putting in behind the scenes to get it done.

There are a lot of benefits to this method. But to get there, you first have to divorce your mind from the strange notion that hours matter.

Hours Don't Matter

When I say hours don't matter, I mean that they do not matter to your client. Of course, hours are a very relevant consideration in terms of managing your own time, so they do come into the equation, but only in a behind-the-scenes and subsidiary way. Because why should your hours matter to your client? Why should they be the definitive factor in your pricing?

When you buy a razor blade at Wal-Mart, do you ask how many hours went into its supply chain? Do you decide on what price you are willing to pay based on the number of those hours? No! You don't care, it doesn't matter. All that matters is the value it provides to you – that it cuts hair. As long as it does its job well, you are willing to pay for it.

The same is true of your client. At the end of the day, for example, if you design a quality website, absolutely no one will ever know or care how many hours it actually took. Will your client's prospective client click on a link solely due to the fact that you billed for x hours of working on it? The real value to your client is ENTIRELY dependent on the quality of the end product and how reliably it engages their users, regardless of how many seconds ticked by while you were keeping track of hours.

Here's another reason it doesn't make sense to charge by hour: the value of each hour is not the same. In economics there is a principle known as the *law of diminishing marginal returns*. If I remember correctly, my dusty college textbook used the example of cheeseburgers, so I'll run with that.

Don't Sell 40 Cheeseburgers to One Person

Say you've hardly eaten all day and are exhausted at the end of a long drive. You see a billboard for McBurger Burgers and cave in, entering with $30 in your pocket. You ask at the counter how much a burger will be.

"You see," is the reply, "we don't have established prices here. It depends on how hungry you are. You look pretty hungry – that will be $15 for you."

You are likely shocked since you are used to everything being priced at fixed rates, and aren't used to a negotiated economy. But when you think of it, the cashier is right – you are very hungry, and a mediocre burger is justifiably worth $15 to you.

So you eat it, and of course are still hungry, and return to the counter.

"Do you have anything cheaper? I'm still fairly hungry, but can't justify $15 again."

"Oh no worries, a second one is only $8."

And so on. Pretty soon you are getting dollar burgers, and you aren't sure if even that's a good deal anymore, until you are so stuffed that an additional burger would have no value to you, if not a negative value. You wouldn't eat another one even on a $5 dare.

It should be fairly easy to see that in an example like this, the first burger is the most valuable one to you – it's the one you need the most, and that you are willing to pay the most for. The second burger – even though it is identical to the first as far as anyone else could tell, and the same amount of work went into producing it – isn't worth quite as much to you. The more you have, the less beneficial an additional one is. The law of diminishing marginal returns.

Flat Fee Freelancer

Now instead of burgers, picture hours. Are all your hours worth the same? In traditional employment you do many tasks, but your employer is paying you equally whether at any given moment you happen to be solving a pressing problem only your skill set can solve, stuck in traffic while trying to meet up with a prospect who really isn't that interested, restocking the soda cooler, or scrolling through an email newsletter with announcements of company babies and photos of cats.

The reality is that some of your hours are much more valuable to your employer than others, and the hourly rate is simply an average that is spread out for convenience. Sure, some of your work consists of easy or mindless tasks that a college intern or robot could do just as well, but your employer has many needs and so you help where you can; and besides, there isn't enough of your most valuable or integral work to fill out 40 hours a week.

As an independent contractor, though, the beauty is you don't have to put in 40 hours a week to one employer. You can laser-focus on only those tasks where you provide the most value to your clients – and then provide that high-value work to as many clients as you can.

Therefore, they don't have to pay you for hours of diminished-value or easily-replaceable work (to be averaged in with the hours of high-value or irreplaceable work). By choosing your own schedule and relationships, *almost all* of your work can be high-value, in which case your work should be charged accordingly. Instead of selling 40 burgers to one person, find 40 hungry people and sell them each one burger.

Keep in mind that since hourly employment rates are built on the "sell 40 burgers to one person" model, if you are operating on a different (and better) model, then if you set an hourly rate, it invites clients to make apples-to-oranges comparisons that are not relevant.

You will still, though, have some hours of work that are higher-value than others, so if you are charging all clients a single hourly rate, some will be paying too much for the value they get and others too little. And as any business owner knows, there are countless work hours that never get billed for but are still necessary, whether troubleshooting those printers or emailing prospective clients or preparing 1099s. How do you measure how much value those hours provide to your clients? Which parts of them should you bill for? Why bother?

So we see there are two main implications of the law of diminishing marginal returns, and the fact that the value of each hour is not the same:

1. Focus your efforts on high-value hours.
2. Charging a single hourly rate may not be the best way to reflect that value – it can get kind of illogical and tricky.

Additional Strikes Against Hours

This touches on a third reason why you should not charge hourly rates – namely, the "messiness" explained above regarding the hard way to change clients' perception of you.

Remember, when an employee is paid an hourly rate, that is only one part of their total compensation, which is only one part of the revenue they generate – and you are charging for your revenue, not your wage. Charging an hourly rate as an independent contractor is just asking for confusion and underpayment – because when people think "hourly rate," they usually think "wage."

A final reason that hourly rates suck so much for freelancers is that they present a conflict of interest (not to mention a hassle) of keeping track of hours.

Are you really being motivated to work efficiently when you would get paid more by muddling through it? If you end up scrolling through a little social media or watching a few YouTube videos along the way, do you include that time, or know how long that time was in the first place? Do you round time up or down? What if you forget to record the time you finished work a few days ago and can't remember when it was? If you run into a client at the store and talk with them about a project for half an hour, or spend time traveling to a place for research but also visit tourist attractions, what time exactly is billable? Is there a chance your competitors are heavily rounding up, or throwing in extra billable hours for fun – and might this have the effect of compressing hourly rates in the market overall, making it harder to get by if you choose to remain one of those who decide to be honest?

    I say: why bother with all those grey areas? Why play that game?

The Project Fee

Hopefully that's enough to convince you that hourly rates aren't necessarily the way to go, despite their ubiquity. What does a project fee look like?

A project fee recognizes the fact that the value to the client is in the end product. It encourages them to think of their own end result, such as how many sales will be generated or what efficiencies are gained (if a business), or what problems will be solved or how much enjoyment they will get (if an individual). It changes the mindset of the conversation by implicitly focusing the discussion on the project itself rather than on you, and on the benefit rather than the cost. Let's look at an example.

Say you are a graphic designer and a local business is interested in hiring you to design a flyer for an event. They'll be handed out as part of packets at a state fair with an estimated 100,000 attendees. You think it might take you about 10 hours to research, coordinate, and design.

Scenario 1:

You tell the local business you charge $20/hour. It's about what you made before at a graphic design company. They compare that with what they paid graphic designers when they previously did it in-house and it seems reasonable to them. You make $200.

Scenario 2:

Flat Fee Freelancer

You've been paying some attention to the hidden costs of being a freelancer, and realize that your hourly rate needs to be bumped considerably, so you suggest $65/hour (and so you figure you might make $650 total). They toss you out the front door because that seems like an outrageous hourly rate to them.

Scenario 3:

You tell the client the project will be $1,000. You show them a few samples of quality work you've done in the past and that have led to measurable success for other clients, with estimates (preferably as part of recommendations from prior clients) of how much value you added. With your subtle prompting, they review mental estimates of how many people in their target audience will see the flyer and quickly realize that the potential sales with a well-crafted pitch are easily many thousands. It's a no brainer. You make $1,000.

Now this is, of course, just one example of many I could have chosen, and you won't always be able to make five times as much with a project fee. But in addition to the potential for much higher income, there are so many advantages of the second scenario:

- You are aligning your own mindset with that of your client by approaching your project in terms of how to maximize their value.
- You are helping your customer to visualize the strategic benefit of working with you as a partner in their growth, rather than seeing you merely as an expense line to minimize.
- You are running your own business as just that: a business, charging enough to cover wages, non-wage compensation, expenses, and profits.
- You aren't inviting tricky conversations or comparisons about hourly wages.

- Finally, there's no worrying about tracking hours, determining which minutes "count," or conflicts of interest related to how efficiently you work. You can get distracted on YouTube all you want, guilt-free (at least as far as billing is concerned).

I should note, you may also want to consider commission-based arrangements in some cases. It is, after all, the ultimate form of results-based compensation, and if you have reason to be confident in your results it could work out very well. Just be sure everything is in writing with no ambiguity as to how commissions are earned, and keep in mind it is often the least predictable form of income!

Setting the Rate

By this point you may be wondering something kind of important: how do you decide what amount to charge?

By "kind of important," I mean, of course, "critically important." This can make or break your business.

I suggest looking at three factors.

First, decide on your bare minimum project rate, based on the time you will spend (this step is for your own benefit, and is NOT something you need to tell your client). You'll need a minimum hourly rate in mind that you are willing to accept.

As you may recall, a rule of thumb you could use it that this rate should be about triple what your minimum rate as an employee would be, based on the fact that an employee's wage is about 69% of total compensation, and that compensation is about half of the employee's output value. Keep in mind though, these are national averages, and based on your industry a higher or lower approximation may be appropriate (likely higher if, say, your line of work requires a lot of investment in equipment or certifications, or if you would get a lot of non-wage compensation as an employee like health insurance or profit-sharing – and lower if not).

Then multiply this rate by an estimate of how many hours the project will take (and round up to account for the time and expenses that aren't directly tied to the project, but are still necessary for your business, such as marketing, technology, accounting, legal, and the portion of your invoiced work that never gets paid). The result will be your minimum project rate.

The rate you use can of course be higher or lower depending on how strongly you actually want to do the project – there's no one magic rate. The idea is to just have realistic expectations of a minimum amount you need to charge to compensate you for your time, as a way of drawing a line in the sand to protect yourself from burning out on projects that would take more time than they are worth.

Second, you will need to consider what your competitors are charging. More on this later. The main thing is that you want to have an idea of where your competitors are at so you can know how to position yourself. You don't necessarily need to match or beat the competition on price – with the value proposition you provide the client, as discussed a few pages ago, you should be putting yourself in a decent position regardless – but you don't want to price yourself completely out of the game.

If competition is charging an hourly rate, you probably have less to be concerned about. You are in a different ballpark than they are, and no one really knows how many hours either they or you will take to complete the project, so any comparison between you will be apples-to-oranges (and you are the orange)!

Last, but certainly not least: estimate the value added to your client. Of course you won't know an exact figure, but you should at least be able to estimate a range (and, depending on the margin of error, you may want to round down a bit since the client still needs to benefit themselves from the transaction).

There are plenty of resources to help determine how much value can be realized to a business by a good website, or article, or consultant, or business plan, or video, or machinery upgrade, or social media engagement. Ask your former clients if they have measured the results of your work. Find friends or connections with experience in the industry and interview them. Google it (and search as if you were in your client's shoes, e.g. "How much could I gain in efficiencies if I hired a consultant for XYZ..."). Factor in the size of your client, and the scope of their market affected by your project – the larger they are, the more they have to gain (or lose) by hiring the right person.

Once you have an idea of these three factors – your personal minimum rate to make it worth your time, what your competition charges, and how much value you could add to your client – setting a rate is straightforward. As long as it is within reason (in light of competition), you are mainly just looking at two figures: your personal minimum rate and the value you can add. Quote the higher of the two.

It's pretty basic. All you are doing is charging what your project is worth to the client, while still setting a floor at how much your time is worth to you.

Because while your client doesn't need to know or care how much time you spend on something, you of course do. If your time is worth more to you than the value the project provides to the client, it still doesn't hurt to quote the former - the worst that happens is they say no (that's better than you running yourself into the ground for pennies).

But if the value the project provides to the client is more than the time is worth to you, then quote an amount close to the value-added. By doing so, you are in fact reflecting the true value of your labor, and are likely to be able to actually stay in business as a freelancer.

Protect Yourself

Now there are a few caveats.

First off, what if your client doesn't want to pay that much? Maybe you over-estimated the value it would add them, or they want to retain higher margins on the project.

No problem, they will negotiate. In fact, you should expect negotiations fairly regularly, as they will likely feel more free to haggle on a project fee than an hourly rate (as the hourly rate implies a rate on your personal worth, and presents the "messiness" noted earlier). It's much simpler and friendlier to negotiate a project fee than an hourly one, and anticipating that is one reason you should start with a quote on the higher end of any gap between your two estimates (the time value to you and the project value to client).

Just don't go below the personal minimum rate you established. Know how to say "no" and walk away if it doesn't make sense for you to do. Having that willingness to walk away is vitally important to any negotiation in the first place – if the other party senses you are desperate, they will have little incentive to agree to a reasonable rate.

What if your competitors are severely undercharging themselves? Unfortunately, this is a common occurrence, and those who underestimate their own value are not only hurting themselves, but the whole industry.

You will probably find that more experienced competitors don't give dirt cheap estimates – as those that do so are usually naively underestimating the time and costs of running a business, and don't last long. But while they do last, they can make it awfully hard for you to charge what you should. If this competition is charging an hourly rate and is new to the game, you may be able to point out to a prospective client that the project may take much longer than your competition is estimating. And as mentioned above, by approaching the table with a results-based standpoint you may be able to stand out regardless of what others are charging.

However, if your flat-fee, value proposition just isn't able to reasonably compete regardless of how you present it, what can you do?

I think we can take a clue from the employee world – talk to your peers! In the 1800s, employees started realizing that individually they couldn't get very far with negotiating rates since no one wanted to be the first to lose their job; but collectively, with unions, they could work out more optimal win-win scenarios.

Now, with unionization long on the decline already, along with the rapid growth of independent freelancers, laborers find themselves more fragmented and in a weaker bargaining position than may be desired. I would highly recommend looking for – or initiating – opportunities to band with other freelancers, whether locally or on the web.

Join Freelancers Union (www.freelancersunion.org), which while not a union in the technical sense, is a great advocacy group that has a lot of resources, including access to group life, health, disability, and liability insurance policies. Find social media "group" pages for indie workers in your industry and/or local area. Meet up with your peers at a coffee shop a few times a year to share stories and ideas – and to set minimum rates. It can certainly be helpful to establish some level of mutual understanding among your competing freelancers so that you don't end up mutually self-destructing by setting rates too low.

Finally, perhaps the biggest risk of charging a flat fee is what if the project ends up taking longer than you anticipated? Especially if you are new to your line of work, this is a very real risk.

A friend of mine is a brilliant computer programmer, and in college he got connected with a company that was looking for someone to build a custom app for them. He knew it would be a sizable project but figured he could do it on the side while in school, and said he would do it for $4,000. Several years later and nearly 2,000 hours later, he finished. He said on the bright side, he learned a lot along the way, but it's probably safe to say one of the things he learned is that it sucks to make $2/hour. Don't let this happen to you.

There are a few precautions you should take to mitigate this risk. First and foremost, make sure you have a reasonable basis for estimating the time a project will actually take when you are setting your personal minimum rate for a project. Track your approximate hours as much as possible, and if you are a novice ask someone who is experienced for their opinion (especially if you are considering taking on a big project). You don't need exact estimates, but you at least need to know on an order of magnitude what you are getting yourself into.

With time you will get fairly good at estimating project lengths to the point it will become second-nature, but you should generally round up when determining your minimum quote so that if it does take a little longer you aren't selling yourself short. However, you do need to accept the risk that there will likely still be a few times that you end up putting in more hours than anticipated, but as long as you are making informed and adaptive estimates (and using a "Scope of Work" as described below!), that risk should be more than compensated for over the long run by the many times you are better off with a project fee than an hourly one.

The other precaution that you absolutely need to take to protect yourself from this risk is a "Scope of Work" document, also known as a "Statement of Work." Not only does this provide common ground on matters such as billing terms and project timelines, but perhaps its most important benefit to you is to account for the risk of the client adding more work once it has already begun.

You don't want someone to take advantage of you by squeezing ever more and more out of you while expecting it all to be covered

Flat Fee Freelancer

by a pre-arranged flat fee (as happened to my friend). This is called "scope creep" and it is as creepy as it sounds – you don't want it.

Make sure you have a clearly-defined Scope of Work in writing beforehand (preferably signed by both parties) that outlines what exactly the project entails and that states that any work requested outside of what is already outlined would be considered and billed as a separate project. Don't let your client get the idea that they can turn you into a "free"-lancer.

Another reason to have some sort of Scope of Work in writing is in order to protect yourself from straight up non-payment. A study by Freelancer's Union of over 5,000 freelancers found that, on average, about 13% of respondents' earned income was never paid out to them.[19] Ouch. Less than a third of respondents said they regularly work under a written agreement.

Scopes of Work don't have to be complicated – for most projects you can type something up that covers the bases in less than an hour, and once you have a template you can probably make tweaks for similar projects in minutes – but for your own sake, please use them.

Conclusion

However many brilliant ideas, diligent hours of work, or good connections you have, it won't mean a thing if you aren't charging enough. Billing an hourly rate similar to what you would make as an employee is about as sure a path to extinction as there is. Project fees will help you and your client to appreciate the full value of what you provide. In the process, you can survive as a freelancer – and perhaps even thrive.

If you are going to freelance, I want you to do it well. Don't sell yourself short. You need to know how much to charge, not only to pay your wages, but also to cover non-wage compensation, business expenses, liabilities, and profits. These factors can quickly add up – running a business is expensive. Remember you are charging revenue, not wages.

Not only do you need to align your mindset with this reality, but you need your clients to be on board as well. You can do this by focusing on the value your project will provide to a client, rather than on the hours you will labor in the process. The hours don't matter to your client. In reality, not every hour represents the same value anyway; focus your time on the highest-value work you can provide, and bill based on that value.

Of course, you still need to factor in your time when setting a rate. Circumstances vary, but you will probably need to be charging enough so that your revenue is around 3 times the wage you would make for the same amount of time as an employee. Primarily negotiate your rate based on the value it adds to your client, but use this as a floor to protect yourself.

Be sure to protect yourself in other ways as well. If competition is running everyone into the ground with low rates, try banding with them. Use Scope of Work agreements, so that you don't end up doing lots of extra work for no additional pay – and so that you get paid in the first place.

If you are starting a business, networks and good advice are invaluable. Join Freelancer's Union. Ask your local Chamber of Commerce or Economic Development Organization for resources. There are many local non-profits that specialize in helping entrepreneurs with everything from mentorship to grant-writing. There are plenty of social media groups where you can connect with similar freelancers. Find people who are experienced and successful in what you do, and ask them for advice. This ventures beyond the scope of this short book, but I wanted to give a shout-out to the fact that there are so many great – and free – resources that will give help to entrepreneurs who are open to receiving it. As I said, I want you to succeed.

Best of luck.

Thanks for reading this. I hope you got a lot out of it.

If you'd like to connect with me and other like-minded entrepreneurs, and get access to free content and ideas on starting and running your own businesses, **join our free Facebook group called "Lifequester Hacks"** (www.facebook.com/groups/lifequesterhacks). I'd love to see you there!

If you think this little book has helped you grow your freelance business more than you previously thought was possible, and would like to help me create more solutions (including a podcast) for entrepreneurs, **check out my Patreon page:** www.patreon.com/stephenpoynter.

Patreon allows you to support me to ensure I can continue creating valuable content for you, while getting access to exclusive content, community, discounts, and events in return. This can include helping to guide the content of my podcast and submitting questions to be answered, monthly group video chats with me, a signed copy of this book, discounts on stays at our vacation rental or trips I lead, and much more! Visit the link above for details.

You can also keep in touch via my:
- website (www.workwithstephenpoynter.com)
- blog (www.notwthhaste.wordpress.com)
- Medium (www.medium.com/@stephenpoynter)
- Instagram (@stephenpoynt)

I'd love to hear from you!

Acknowledgements

I'm grateful to the writing community of Grand Marais, MN for their friendship and support. I probably wouldn't have gotten around to finishing this book if it weren't for the weekly writing group times. Thank you Steve and Brian for your stories, and Dale for your excellent editorial eye. Courtney Whalen, as always, has shown that she has some sort of superhuman gene. Most of all, I'm grateful to Rae, without whom I would never have started writing at all.

About the Author

Stephen Poynter is an author, freelancer, lifestyle entrepreneur, world traveler, and audiobook narrator with a professional background and degree in finance. As a rule, he loves anything that is meaningful, thought-provoking, well-crafted, or related to the human journey. Originally hailing from Eau Claire, WI, he spends a lot of his time up at a tiny house he built in the woods of Northern Minnesota near Grand Marais, where he and his wife Rae (also an author) run a vacation rental business and work on their creative endeavors.

Endnotes

---

[1] There are of course many resources out there on finding and developing your skillset, business plan, and market. I might suggest starting with a local small business or economic development organization. A few online publications that I find have good content are Medium (https://medium.com/topic/freelancing) and The Balance Small Business (https://www.thebalancesmb.com/small-business-info-4161643). There are also companies like Pryor Learning that offer excellent in-person seminars and online webinars, and while these are often more tailored toward corporate clients there are many such sessions that are still relevant to starting a business.

[2] That is, those who weren't in some form of forced servitude, which was probably most of them – but otherwise you might have sold your extra produce or clothes you made in the market, or were an apprentice and then set up your own shop, or transported goods for someone while on your own journey for a fee, or tutored for well-off families, etc.

[3] PYMTS.com, "The Gig Economy Index," April 2019, https://www.pymnts.com/wp-content/uploads/2019/04/Gig-Economy-April-19.pdf.

[4] Ibid.

[5] Abdullahi Muhammed, "Busting The Gig Economy Myths: 40% Of Gig Workers Now Earn Six-Figures Per Year," Forbes (Forbes Magazine, June 1, 2019), https://www.forbes.com/sites/abdullahimuhammed/2019/06/01/busting-the-gig-economy-myths-40-of-gig-workers-now-earn-six-figures-per-year/#534739864542.

[6] Sam Sabin, "In Robust Job Market, Gig Workers' Satisfaction on Par With Wider Workforce," Morning Consult, September 18, 2018, https://morningconsult.com/2018/09/18/in-robust-job-market-gig-workers-satisfaction-par-wider-workforce/.

[7] Board of Governors of the Federal Reserve System, "Report on the Economic Well-Being of U.S. Households in 2018," May 2019, https://www.federalreserve.gov/publications/files/2018-report-economic-well-being-us-households-201905.pdf. (The 2019 report did not include updated figures for the relevant data point here).

[8] Economic Policy Institute, "Uber Drivers Earn the Equivalent of $9.21 in Hourly Wages: Uber and Other Gig Platforms Account for Far Less of the Economy than Many Estimates Suggest," Economic Policy Institute, May 18, 2018, https://www.epi.org/press/uber-drivers-earn-the-equivalent-of-9-21-in-hourly-wages-uber-and-other-gig-platforms-account-for-far-less-of-the-economy-than-many-estimates-suggest/.

[9] PYMTS.com, "The Gig Economy Index."
See also:
Nathan Gibson, "Six-Figure Earners Are a Growing Share of U.S. 'Gig' Workforce," Employee or Independent Contractor?, July 10, 2017, https://nathansgibson.org/six-figure-earners-growing-share-u-s-gig-workforce/.

[10] Greg Jensen et al., "Peak Profit Margins? A US Perspective" (Bridgewater Associates, LP, February 17, 2019), https://www.bridgewater.com/research-library/daily-observations/

peak-profit-margins-a-us-perspective/peak-profit-margins-a-us-perspective.pdf.

[11] James Manyika et al., "A New Look at the Declining Labor Share of Income in the United States," McKinsey & Company, May 22, 2019, Exhibit 1, https://www.mckinsey.com/featured-insights/employment-and-growth/a-new-look-at-the-declining-labor-share-of-income-in-the-united-states.
See also:
Federal Reserve Bank of St. Louis, "Shares of Gross Domestic Income: Compensation of Employees, Paid: Wage and Salary Accruals: Disbursements: To Persons," FRED Economic Data, August 29, 2019, https://fred.stlouisfed.org/series/W270RE1A156NBEA.
Federal Reserve Bank of St. Louis, "Business Sector: Labor Share," FRED Economic Data, May 7, 2020, https://fred.stlouisfed.org/series/PRS84006173.

[12] Though unemployment benefits have recently been opened to freelancers as part of emergency relief legislation. It will be interesting to see if this is temporary, or lasts as part of broader awareness of freelancing; though I suspect that if it does last freelancers would have to start paying into unemployment taxes just as employers do.
See also:
Alison Doyle, "Collecting Unemployment Benefits for Self-Employed Workers," The Balance Careers, May 7, 2020, https://www.thebalancecareers.com/can-i-collect-unemployment-if-i-m-self-employed-2064148.

[13] U.S. Bureau of Labor Statistics, "Employer Costs For Employee Compensation – December 2010," March 19, 2020, https://www.bls.gov/news.release/pdf/ecec.pdf.

[14] Manyika et al., "A New Look at the Declining Labor Share of Income in the United States."

[15] Joe Hadzima, "How Much Does An Employee Cost?," Boston Business Journal, n.d., https://web.mit.edu/e-club/hadzima/how-much-does-an-employee-cost.html.

[16] "Employment Cost Trends - ECT Tables," U.S. Bureau of Labor Statistics, n.d., https://www.bls.gov/ncs/ect/#tables. (Look for "Employer Costs for Employee Compensation" under Data Tables). "Labor Productivity and Costs - LPC Tables and Charts," U.S. Bureau of Labor Statistics, n.d., https://www.bls.gov/lpc/. (Look for "Labor Productivity and Cost Measures" under Data Tables, especially "Industries (Interactive)").

[17] And remember to deduct those expenses when you file taxes! Employers aren't taxed on all of their revenues, and neither should you be.

[18] Society for Human Resource Management, "2017 Human Capital Benchmarking Report," December 2017, pg 6 "Revenue per FTE", https://www.shrm.org/hr-today/trends-and-forecasting/research-and-surveys/Documents/2017-Human-Capital-Benchmarking.pdf.

[19] Freelancers Union, "The Costs of Nonpayment: A Study on Nonpayment and Late Payment in the Freelance Workforce," December 10, 2015, https://fu-web-prod-media.s3.amazonaws.com/content/advocacy/uploads/resources/FU_NonpaymentReport_r3.pdf.